# BODY PARTS

## Grow a bilingual vocabulary by:

- **Looking** at pictures and words
- **Talking** about what you see
- **Touching** and naming objects
- **Using** questions to extend learning...
  Ask questions that invite children
    to share information.
  Begin your questions with words like...
    who, what, when, where and how.

## Desarrolle su vocabulario bilingüe:

- **Mire** los dibujos y las palabras
- **Hable** de lo que ves
- **Toque** y nombre objetos
- **Use** preguntas para aumentar el aprendizaje...
  Use preguntas que invitan a
    los niños a compartir la información.
  Empiece sus frases con el uso de estas palabras...
    ¿quién? ¿qué? ¿cuándo? ¿por dónde? y ¿cómo?

**Learning Props, L.L.C.**

# PARTES DEL CUERPO

# head  la cabeza

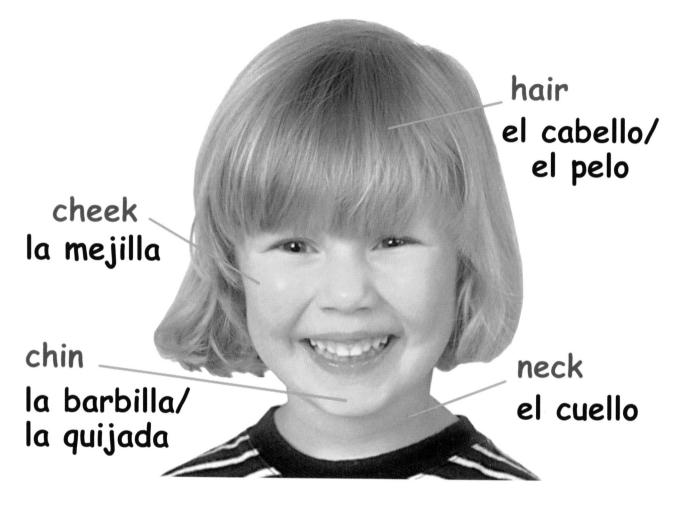

hair
**el cabello/ el pelo**

cheek
**la mejilla**

chin
**la barbilla/ la quijada**

neck
**el cuello**

# face  la cara

eye
el ojo

skin
la piel

mouth
la boca

forehead
la frente

ear
la oreja

nose
la nariz

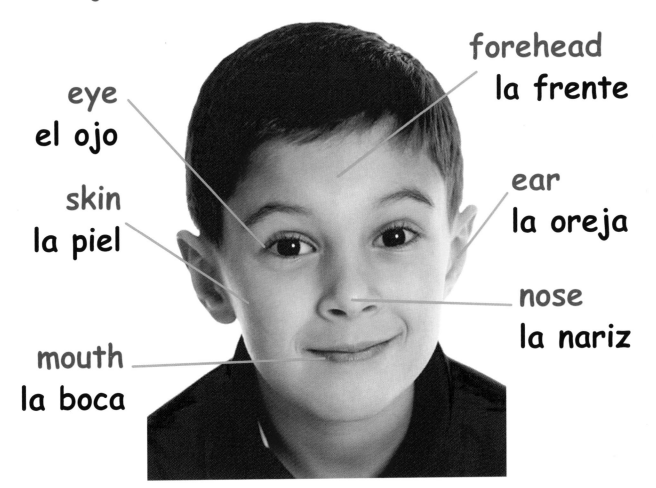

# eye   el ojo

eyebrow
la ceja

eyelashes
las pestañas

eyelid
el párpado

pupil
la pupila

iris
el iris

# ear   la oreja

earlobe

**el lóbulo de la oreja**

# mouth   la boca

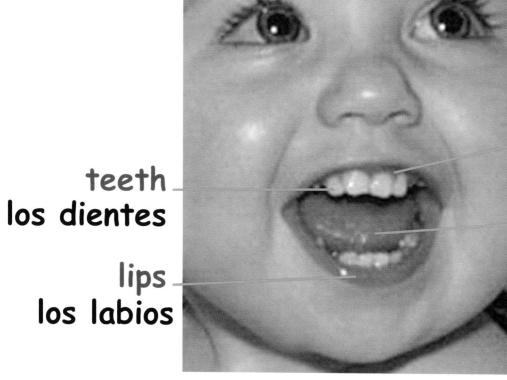

teeth
los dientes

lips
los labios

gums
las encias

tongue
la lengua

# hair el cabello/el pelo

**red hair**
**el cabello rojo/**
**el pelo rojo**

**black hair**
**el cabello negro/**
**el pelo negro**

**blonde hair**
**el cabello rubio/**
**el pelo rubio**

**brown hair**
**el cabello castaño/**
**el pelo castaño**

**curly hair**
**el cabello**
**rizado/**
**el pelo**
**rizado**

**straight hair**
**el cabello liso/el cabello lacio/**
**el pelo liso/el pelo lacio**

# nose la nariz

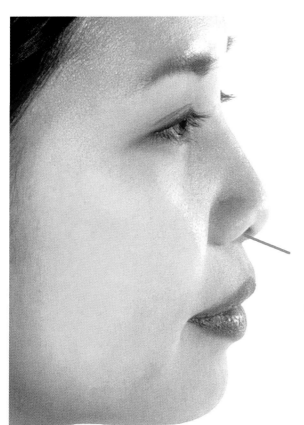

nostril
**la ventana de la nariz/
el hueco de la nariz**

# arm   el brazo

**hand**
**la mano**

**elbow**
**el codo**

**shoulder**
**el hombro**

**wrist**
**la muñeca**

# hand   la mano

fingers
los
dedos
de la
mano

thumb
el pulgar

fingernail
la uña

knuckle
el nudillo

palm
la palma

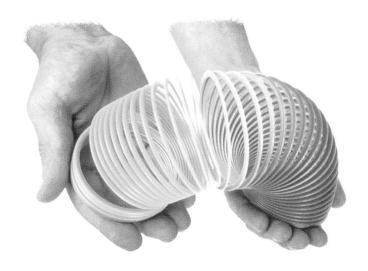

# leg  la pierna

foot
el pie

ankle
el tobillo

shin
la espinilla

thigh
el muslo

knee
la rodilla

hip
la cadera

# foot   el pie

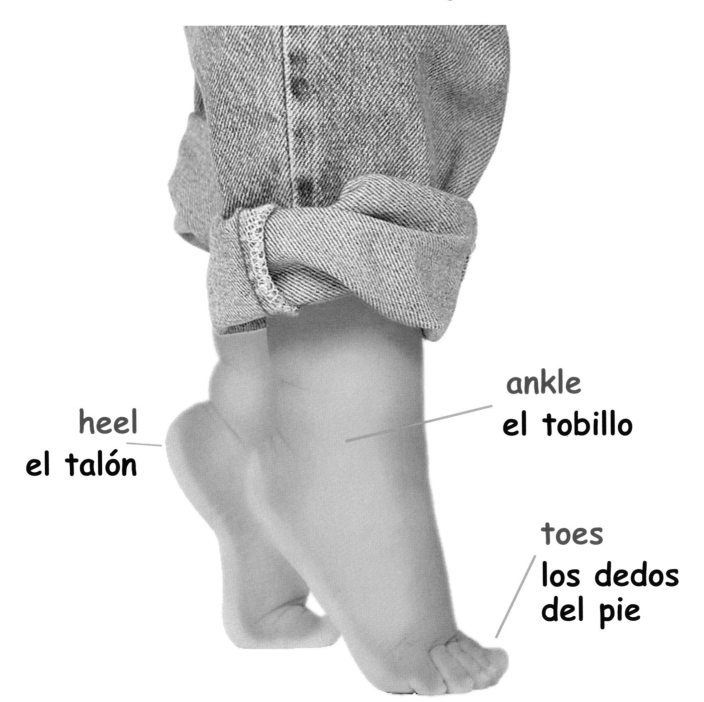

heel
el talón

ankle
el tobillo

toes
los dedos
del pie

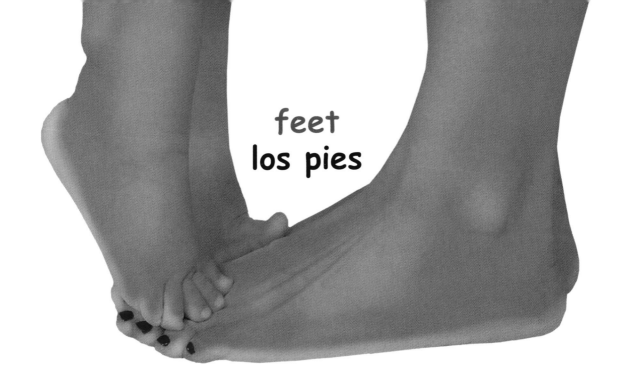

feet
los pies

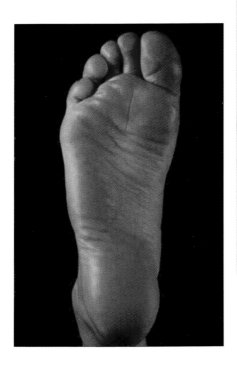

elbow
el codo

shoulder
el hombro

chest
el pecho

stomach
el estómago

waist
la cintura

hip
la cadera

chest
el pecho

back
la espalda

bottom
el trasero

# Which body parts can you name?

# ¿Puedes indicar las partes del cuerpo?

# Which body parts can you name on these animals?

# ¿Puedes indicar las partes del cuerpo de estos animales?

# pronunciation

head/**hed**                          la cabeza/lah kah-**bay**-sah
hair/**hair**                          el cabello, el pelo/ehl kah-**bay**-yoh, ehl **pay**-lo
neck/**nek**                          el cuello/ehl **kweh**-yoh
chin/**chin**                          la barbilla, la quijada/
                                        lah bahr-**bee**-yah, lah key-**ha**-dah

cheek/**cheek**                      la mejilla/lah may-**hee**-yah
face/**fayss**                        la cara/lah **kah**-rah
forehead/**for**-hed              la frente/lah **fren**-tay
ear/**ihr**                            la oreja/lah ore-**ray**-ha
nose/**nohz**                        la nariz/lah nah-**rees**
mouth/**mouth**                    la boca/lah **boh**-kah
skin/**skin**                          la piel/lah pee-**yail**
eye/**eye**                            el ojo/ehl **oh**-hoe
eyelid/**eye**-lid                    el párpado/ehl **pahr**-pah-doe
pupil/**pyoo**-puhl                la pupila/lah poo-**pee**-lah
iris/**eye**-riss                       el iris/ehl **ee**-rees
eyelashes/**eye**-lash-es        las pestañas/lahs pace-**stahn**-yahs
eyebrow/**eye**-brou              la ceja/lah **say**-ha
earlobe/**ihr**-loab                el lóbulo de la oreja/ehl **low**-boo-low day lah ore-**ray**-ha
gums/**guhms**                      las encias/lahs ehn-**see**-yahs
tongue/**tuhng**                    la lengua/lah **len**-gwa
lips/**lips**                            los labios/loase **lah**-bee-owes
teeth/**teeTH**                      los dientes/loase dee-**ehn**-tays
black hair/**blak hair**          el cabello negro, el pelo negro/ehl kah-**bay**-yoh **nay**-grow,
                                        ehl **pay**-lo **nay**-grow
blonde hair/**blond hair**      el cabello rubio, el pelo rubio/ehl kah-**bay**-yoh **roo**-bee-owe,
                                        ehl **pay**-lo **roo**-bee-owe
curly hair/**kur**-lee **hair**    el cabello rizado, el pelo rizado/ehl kah-**bay**-yoh ree-**sah**-doe,
                                        ehl **pay**-lo ree-**sah**-doe
straight hair/**strayt hair**    el cabello liso, el cabello lacio/ehl kah-**bay**-yoh **leese**-owe,
                                        ehl kah-**bay**-owe **lah**-see-owe /
                                        el pelo liso, el pelo lacio/
                                        ehl **pay**-lo **leese**-owe, ehl **pay**-lo **lah**-see-owe
brown hair/**broun hair**       el cabello castaño, el pelo castaño/ehl kah-**bay**-yoh kah-**stah**-nyo,
                                        ehl **pay**-lo kah-**stah**-nyo
red hair/**red hair**              el cabello rojo, el pelo rojo/ehl kah-**bay**-yoh **roe**-hoe,
                                        ehl **pay**-lo **roe**-hoe